SCIENCE FILES

LIGHT

SCIENCE FILES – LIGHT
was produced by

David West 🧍🧍 **Children's Books**
7 Princeton Court
55 Felsham Road
London SW15 1AZ

Designer: Gary Jeffrey
Editor: Gail Bushnell
Picture Research: Carlotta Cooper

First published in Great Britain by Heinemann
Library, Halley Court, Jordan Hill, Oxford
OX2 8EJ, part of Harcourt Education.
Heinemann is a registered trademark
of Harcourt Education Ltd.

08 07 06 05
10 9 8 7 6 5 4 3 2 1

ISBN 0 431 14317 X (HB)
ISBN 0 431 14324 2 (PB)

British Library Cataloguing in Publication Data

Parker, Steve
Light. - (Science files)
1. Light - Juvenile literature 2. Light - Experiments -
Juvenile literature
I. Title
535

PHOTO CREDITS :
Abbreviations: t-top, m-middle, b-bottom, r-right,
l-left, c-centre.

Front cover - tr - Corbis Images, br - Digital Stock.
Pages 3 & 25t, 7t, 10, 14l, 17t, 19br, 29t - Digital
Stock. 4–5 & 21, 6–7, 8t, 27br - Corbis Images.
8b - Andrew Cooper/ Nature Picture Library. 9tl,
13t - DPMU0399 Images @ 1999 Photodisc, Inc.
11 - Rex Features Ltd. 12 - Robert Harding Picture
Library. 15 - European Southern Observatory
(ESO). 16, 25b - The Culture Archive. 22–23 -
The Kobal Collection. 27tl - National Oceanic &
Atmospheric Administration (NOAA). 29bl -
@ BAE Systems Photo Library 2000.

Every effort has been made to contact copyright
holders of any material reproduced in this book.
Any omissions will be rectified in subsequent
printings if notice is given to the publishers.

With special thanks to the models: Felix Blom,
Tucker Bryant and Margaux Monfared.

Printed and bound in China

*An explanation of difficult words can be
found in the glossary on page 31.*

SCIENCE FILES

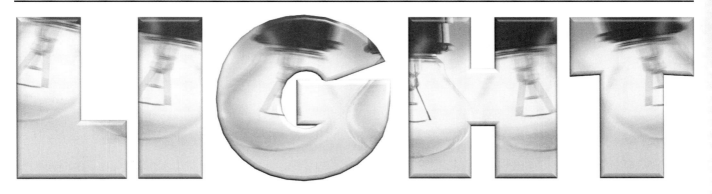

LIGHT

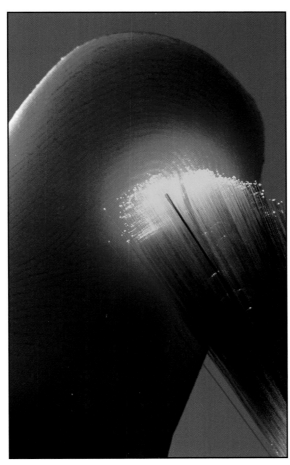

Steve Parker

Heinemann
LIBRARY

CONTENTS

WARNING!
All projects should be supervised by a responsible adult. Some need extra care and expert help, and are marked with a red box. Make sure the instructions are followed. *Never take risks.*

INTRODUCTION

Light is many different things. It can be bright or dim, and white and coloured at the same time! It seems to be everywhere as it shines on us and our surroundings. Yet it also carries telephone, computer and internet information halfway around the world in a split second, along fibres thinner than hairs. In fact light has the fastest speed in the Universe. It is also a form of energy which plants capture to grow. We eat plants, so we too are light-powered.

How it **WORKS**

These panels explain the science behind the projects, and the processes and principles that we see every day, but which we may not always understand!

PROJECT PANEL

The projects are simple to do with supervision, using household items. Remember – scientists are cautious.

They prepare equipment thoroughly, they know what should happen, and they *always* put safety first.

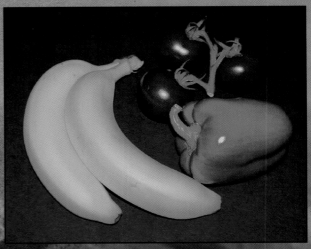

You can read these words, and see what is happening around you, because of light. Light illuminates our world and allows us to carry out our daily lives.

LIGHT AS ENERGY

Light is a form of energy known as electromagnetic energy. It is made of a combination of electrical and magnetic energy, and it travels in straight lines as up-and-down waves known as light rays. Light is not the only form of electromagnetic or EM waves – there is a wide range or spectrum of them, as shown on the opposite page.

The stars in the Universe (right) are gigantic fiery balls of gas that disperse vast quantities of electromagnetic radiation into space.

Normal 'white' light is not just one single type of electromagnetic wave. It is a mixture of many different wavelengths, and each length of wave has a different colour (left).

How it **WORKS**

All the rays and waves shown here are electromagnetic energy. The difference is the lengths of their waves. Longest are radio waves, where one wave can be many hundreds of metres in length.

Light waves are shorter, with thousands packed into one millimetre. Gamma and cosmic rays are shortest, with billions in less than one millimetre.

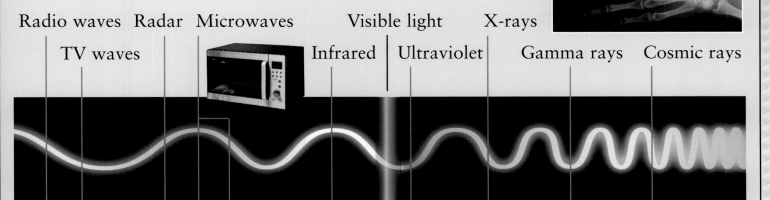

Radio waves   Radar   Microwaves   Visible light   X-rays

TV waves   Infrared | Ultraviolet   Gamma rays   Cosmic rays

LIGHT AND DARK

Darkness is the absence of light. A dark area where light is blocked from falling on an object is known as a shadow. The upright part or gnomon of a sundial casts a shadow that moves around the dial as the Sun moves across the sky, so we can tell the time.

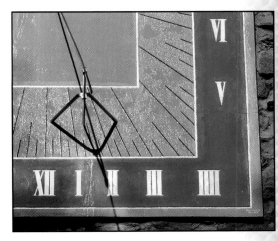

Sundials were used to tell the time over 4000 years ago.

Light shines through the glass, but not the metal on this window.

TRANSPARENT AND OPAQUE

A substance which does not allow light to pass through it, like wood, steel or pottery, is known as opaque. A substance that does allow light through, such as air, water or glass, is called transparent.

7

Light is one of the main forms of energy in the whole Universe. The vastness of space is dotted with giant glowing stars. One of these is relatively near to us and provides the light we rely on every day – the Sun.

Each tiny pinprick of light in the night sky is a star, millions of times bigger than Earth, but also billions of kilometres away. Of all these stars only the Sun, 150 million kilometres away, appears as a burning sphere.

A glow-worm's light is created by the reaction of two chemicals. This female beetle glows to attract a male.

NATURAL LIGHT

The Sun 'burns' the substance hydrogen to form another lightweight gas, helium. As it does so, it gives off vast amounts of electromagnetic energy, including heat (infrared) and light. This takes about eight minutes to reach our planet, as the Sun brightens our world at dawn every day. There are also natural light sources here on Earth. They vary from the flames of wildfires to eerie glow-in-the-dark life-forms, such as jellyfish in the seas, worms on land, and fireflies in the sky.

ARTIFICIAL LIGHT

The Sun is our main light source by day. At night, or inside buildings, subways and similar places, we need to make our own light. In former times people used the flames of lamps and candles, which burned fuels such as natural waxes and oils. Today the vast majority of artificial lights use electrical energy, including filament bulbs and fluorescent tubes.

Household bulbs contain the gas argon, not air, so the filament does not burn out.

Street lamps are yellow in colour because they use sodium vapour bulbs.

MAKING A FILAMENT GLOW

To battery

Protective jar

Filament

From a pad of steel wool, extract one strand as a filament. Twist it around a pencil to make a coil. Wrap its ends around two thick metal wires to hold it up. Cover with a jar for protection. Connect the two thicker wires to a 9-volt battery and the filament should glow for a second or two before it burns out.

WARNING Ensure a qualified adult helps with this project. Always place the jar over the filament before making the connections and disconnect the filament and allow it to cool before handling.

How it WORKS

In a filament or incandescent lamp, electricity forces its way through a very thin wire – the filament. The wire resists the flow, heats up and glows or incandesces, giving off light. A glass bulb covers the filament for protection and contains a special gas, rather than ordinary air, so the filament does not burn away (as it does here).

Most objects around us do not make their own light. We can see them because light bounces or reflects off them into our eyes.

The lake's very smooth water surface acts as a mirror and reflects light rays from around it, into our eyes. We see a mirror-image of the mountains and trees reflected in the lake.

MIRROR-IMAGES

Most objects have rough, dull surfaces. They reflect light from a light source, such as the Sun or an electric lamp, but in a random and haphazard way. Light bounces off very smooth, flat, shiny surfaces in a more accurate and organized way. These surfaces reflect a clear picture of what is in front of them, which we call a mirror-image or 'reflection'.

How it **WORKS**

When light reaches our eyes from an object, we assume it has come in a straight line from the object, because that is what usually happens. So reflected light seems to represent a second version, the mirror-image, of the original object.

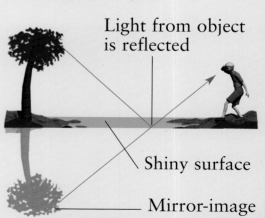

Light from object is reflected

Shiny surface

Mirror-image

SEEING ROUND CORNERS

Devices with very smooth surfaces, usually shiny metal protected by glass, that produce clear reflections are called mirrors. They have many uses, not only for checking our appearance, but in optical (light-based) equipment like cameras, and for rear-view mirrors in vehicles. Two mirrors can bounce light around a solid object so we can 'see round corners'.

Periscopes allow people to see at a higher level than their line of vision. Submarines use them to look above the water level and see the surface.

MAKE A PERISCOPE

This periscope is a long cardboard box with an opening near the top, and another on the opposite side near the bottom. Two mirrors are placed facing each other at 45° at top and bottom. Periscopes can be useful in big crowds, to see over people's heads.

How it WORKS

The two mirrors are angled at 45°. Light rays from the object bounce off the upper mirror, travel down to the lower mirror, and reflect off this into the eyes.

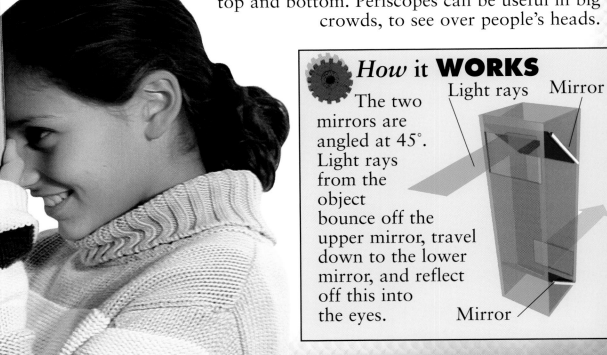

Light rays   Mirror

Mirror

Light does not always travel in straight lines. When it passes into a clear or see-through substance, its path may be angled or bent. This bending is known as refraction – and it is amazingly useful.

REFRACTED LIGHT

When light waves pass from one transparent substance to another, they change speed and bend or refract. Usually, the greater the difference in density (heaviness) between the two substances, the greater the angle of refraction. We can see refraction when we look at objects in a glass container or when hot air creates a mirage.

In this mirage in the Sahara Desert, the thin blue line just below the horizon is actually a strip of sky!

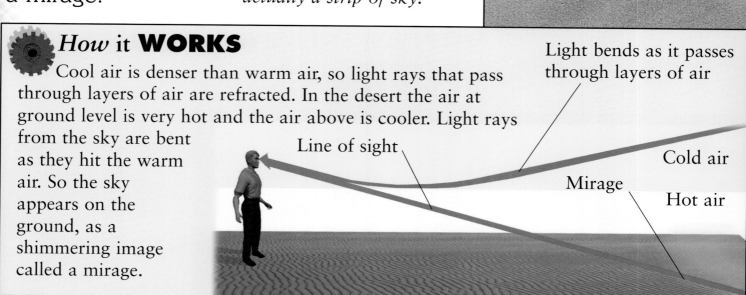

How it WORKS

Cool air is denser than warm air, so light rays that pass through layers of air are refracted. In the desert the air at ground level is very hot and the air above is cooler. Light rays from the sky are bent as they hit the warm air. So the sky appears on the ground, as a shimmering image called a mirage.

Light bends as it passes through layers of air

Line of sight

Cold air

Mirage

Hot air

ILLUSIONS OF REFRACTION

Refraction makes water, in a pond or swimming pool, seem shallower. Light rays from the bottom are bent at a slight downward angle as they pass from the water up into air. However we assume the rays are straight and so we see the bottom as nearer than it really is. Refraction has hundreds of uses, especially in the curved or bulging pieces of glass or plastic called lenses.

Light rays from the fish are refracted when they pass from the water to the glass bowl and then as they go from the bowl into the air.

How it **WORKS**

Objects in water look closer to the surface when you look down on them, because the light rays that are reflected by them are bent as they leave the water.

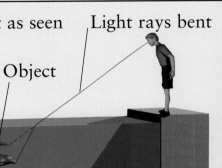

Object as seen   Light rays bent

Object

MAKE A SIMPLE LENS

Fill a round bowl with water and shine a powerful torch through two narrow slits in a card, into the water. Adjust the angle of the beams, and see how they bend as they pass in and out of the water.

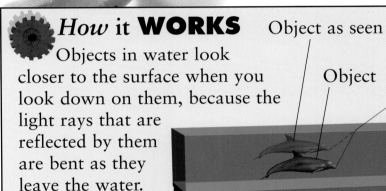

Lenses are specially shaped pieces of clear glass or plastic, which refract or bend light rays in a precise way, to change the view of objects seen through them. They are very common – there's one in each of your eyes!

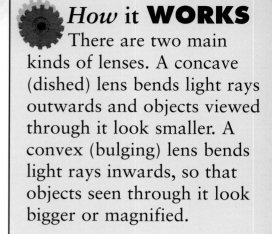

How it WORKS

There are two main kinds of lenses. A concave (dished) lens bends light rays outwards and objects viewed through it look smaller. A convex (bulging) lens bends light rays inwards, so that objects seen through it look bigger or magnified.

BIGGER AND BIGGER

A microscope can make tiny objects look more than 1000 times larger. It usually has two lenses, both convex. The one at the bottom nearest the object is small but well-rounded and powerful, with a short focal length. It produces a magnified image. This is enlarged further by the other lens at the top of the tube, called the eyepiece lens. Light microscopes are used for magnifications of up to 2000 times.

Binocular microscopes have two sets of tubes and lenses, one for each eye.

MAKE A MAGNIFIER

A drop of water forms itself into a rounded shape which can be used as a convex lens, to magnify small objects. However this water-drop lens has a short focal length. So you have to place the object, or specimen, and your eye quite close to it.

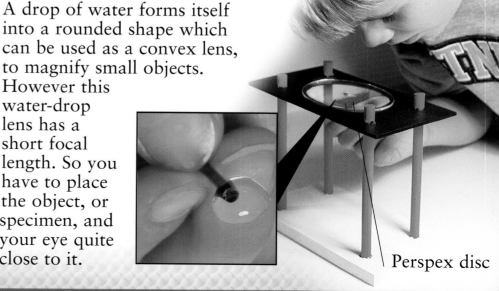

Perspex disc

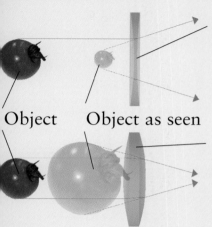

A concave lens angles light rays outwards. The object seems to be smaller.

Object   Object as seen

A convex lens angles light rays inwards. The object seems to be larger.

How it **WORKS**

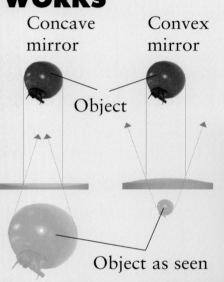

Mirrors work in the opposite way to lenses. A concave mirror will make objects seem larger and a convex mirror will make objects look smaller.

Concave mirror   Convex mirror

Object

Object as seen

NEARER AND NEARER

A refracting (lens-based) telescope is similar to a microscope. It usually has two convex lenses. These are different in size and refracting power to those in the microscope. The objective lens pointing up to the sky is large, with a long focal length, and the eyepiece lens is smaller, with a short focal length. The world's largest telescopes are reflecting telescopes, with a concave mirror rather than an objective lens.

This concave mirror 8.2 metres across will be one of four in the Very Large Telescope (VLT) at the Paranal Observatory, Chile. It takes two years to polish each mirror perfectly smooth.

The camera obscura had a lens in one side. Light shone through the lens and was reflected by a mirror on to a surface to form an image of the outside scene.

As we look around, our eyes receive millions of light waves every second. The eye sends nerve signals to the brain, where we form a continuous picture of our surroundings.

FORMING AN IMAGE

To see a clear, unblurred view, light rays from the surroundings must be brought together in one place to form a sharp picture or image. This is called focusing. In cameras, microscopes and telescopes it is done using lenses. Some cameras focus their images on to a layer of light-sensitive chemicals, called photographic film. The chemicals change according to the amount and colour of light hitting them, forming a photograph.

PINHOLE CAMERA

Cut a 'window' in one side of a large cardboard box and tape tracing paper into it. Make a tiny pinhole in the middle of the opposite side. Hold the box facing a bright light source to see the image on the tracing paper.

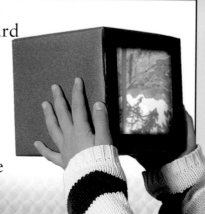

How it WORKS

Light rays pass through the tiny hole, which acts as a lens, and form an image on the paper. The image is upside down, since light rays from high up angle down and shine on the lower part of the paper.

Light rays

Upside down image

LIGHT TO ELECTRIC SIGNALS

Digital cameras work in a very similar way to our eyes. Both have small holes to let light shine in on to an area where the image is focused. They have an image-capturing device which creates electric signals that can be sent to a computer or the brain.

A camera lens is visible, but the eye lens is in the dark interior of the pupil. The eye's coloured iris controls the amount of light, like the camera's aperture control.

How it WORKS

Inside the eye, the light from the image is focused on to the back of the retina. This has over 120 million tiny sensors. These make nerve impulses which are sent through the optic nerve to the brain.

In a digital camera, the image is focused on to a microchip. This has millions of pixels that capture the image. This is sent along a cable to a mini-computer.

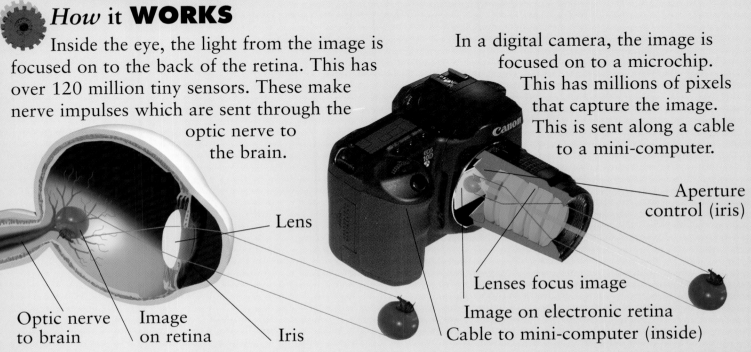

Lens

Aperture control (iris)

Lenses focus image

Optic nerve to brain

Image on retina

Iris

Image on electronic retina
Cable to mini-computer (inside)

17

Most of the light we see and use each day, from the Sun or electric lamps, is known as 'white' light. But white light is not a single colour. In fact it is all colours added together.

Rainbows occur when sunlight shines through raindrops. The seven colours that appear are red, orange, yellow, green, blue, indigo and violet.

RAINBOW COLOURS

The colour of light depends on the length of its waves, as explained earlier (page 6). The longest are red, medium-length waves are green, and the shortest are violet. Between these colours are many others – in fact, millions. The full range is called the visible spectrum. For everyday use we usually simplify it to seven, known as the colours of the rainbow.

How it WORKS

'White' light like sunlight is a mixture of all colours. Raindrops work like tiny lenses to refract and split light into all the colours of the spectrum, which we see as a rainbow.

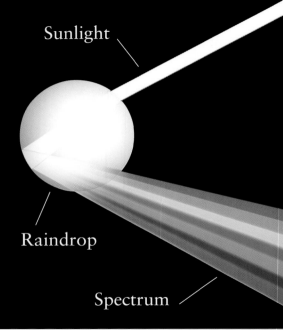

Sunlight

Raindrop

Spectrum

How it WORKS

When the three primary light colours all shine together at the same place, their different wavelengths combine to produce the full range of wavelengths, which we see as 'white' light.

MAKING WHITE LIGHT FROM COLOURS

You can show how white light is a mixture of colours, using the three primary colours of light. You need three torches, each with a cardboard tube to make the beam narrower. At the end of each tube place a colour filter, such as a piece of tinted see-through plastic, to alter the beam. In dark conditions, shine the torch beams down, aiming them so that all three colours overlap on the central area.

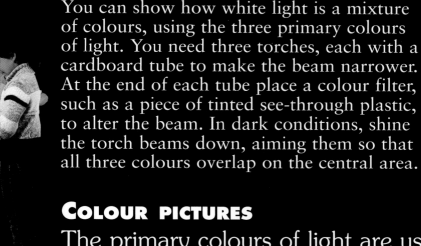

Green filter

Red filter

Blue filter

COLOUR PICTURES

The primary colours of light are used on a television screen, as groups of tiny glowing spots called pixels. If just the red dots glow in one area of the screen, that area looks red. If green and red glow, the eye merges them to see yellow. If all three colours glow, it looks white.

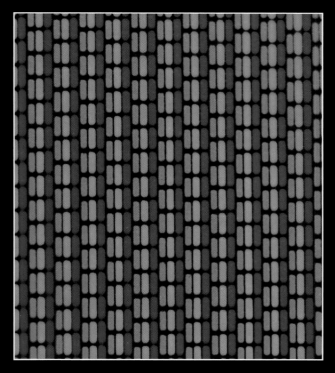

A television or computer screen seen close up shows the three primary colours of green, red and blue.

19

Why are tomatoes red, bananas yellow and peppers green? These foods do not give out their own coloured light. Their colours depend on which light waves they absorb and which they reflect.

WHY THINGS HAVE COLOURS

Ordinary 'white' light illuminating an object contains all the colours of the spectrum. However not all the colours bounce or reflect off the object – some are absorbed. It is the colours that are reflected which create what we see. The colours absorbed or reflected depend on the detailed structure of the object's surface, including microscopic bumps, pits and ridges.

How it WORKS

A ripe tomato soaks up, or absorbs, all colours except red, which is reflected back into our eyes.

White light

Red light waves

SUBTRACTING WAVELENGTHS

Without filter

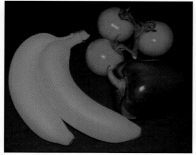

Red filter

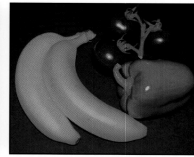

Green filter

Filters can subtract light waves as they reflect back to our eyes. The red filter makes the pepper black by blocking green light waves, while the green filter makes the tomatoes darker.

MIXING COLOURS

Pigments, dyes, inks, paints and stains are substances with strong colours. They work by absorbing most colours of light, leaving just a few. The three primary colours of pigments are cyan, magenta and yellow. These three colours can be used to make all other colours, when they are mixed together in various different combinations.

Artists spend much time mixing pigments to create the right shade or hue for their paintings.

Yellow

Red

Green

Black

Cyan

Blue

Magenta

Where two of the three primary colours of pigments overlap, they form the primary colours of light – green, blue and red. Where all three overlap, they absorb all colours of light and the result is black.

THE PRINTED PAGE

When pictures are printed, only the three primary pigment colours of ink are used. The picture is made up of many tiny dots, each one of these colours. The eye cannot see individual dots and 'blurs' their colours together to make all the others.

The three pigment colours merge together in different combinations to make all the colours of the spectrum.

21

When we go to the movies or watch television, the pictures we see on the screen are not really moving. They are still, like photographs. So why do they seem to move?

FASTER FLICKERS

The reason is the way our eyes work. In ordinary light the eye takes about one-tenth of a second to form an image of a scene and send its nerve signals to the brain, before it is ready for the next image. So the eye could pick out five images shown in one second, as flicking from one to the next. Above 15 or so per second, the images merge or fuse into each other as a moving image. Cinema film shows 24 images per second, and television more, so we see an impression of smooth motion.

Before cinema, English photographer Eadweard Muybridge experimented with putting many cameras in a row to take photographs of a moving animal.

A movie camera records its many still images, or frames, on a long reel of photographic film wound inside a round case.

How it **WORKS**

As a slot rotates past your eyes, you see a split-second view of the pictures through it, reflected in the mirror. By the time the next slot comes past, the pictures have moved slightly. This happens too fast for your eyes to see the images separately, so they merge.

PRAXINOSCOPE

The praxinoscope was an early and simple version of the movies, and very popular in its day. Copy the design below, or create your own, on a disc of stiff card. Cut out the slots carefully.

Spin the disc on a central pivot, such as a pencil or piece of wooden dowel with the images facing a mirror about half a metre away. Look through the slots to see the moving images.

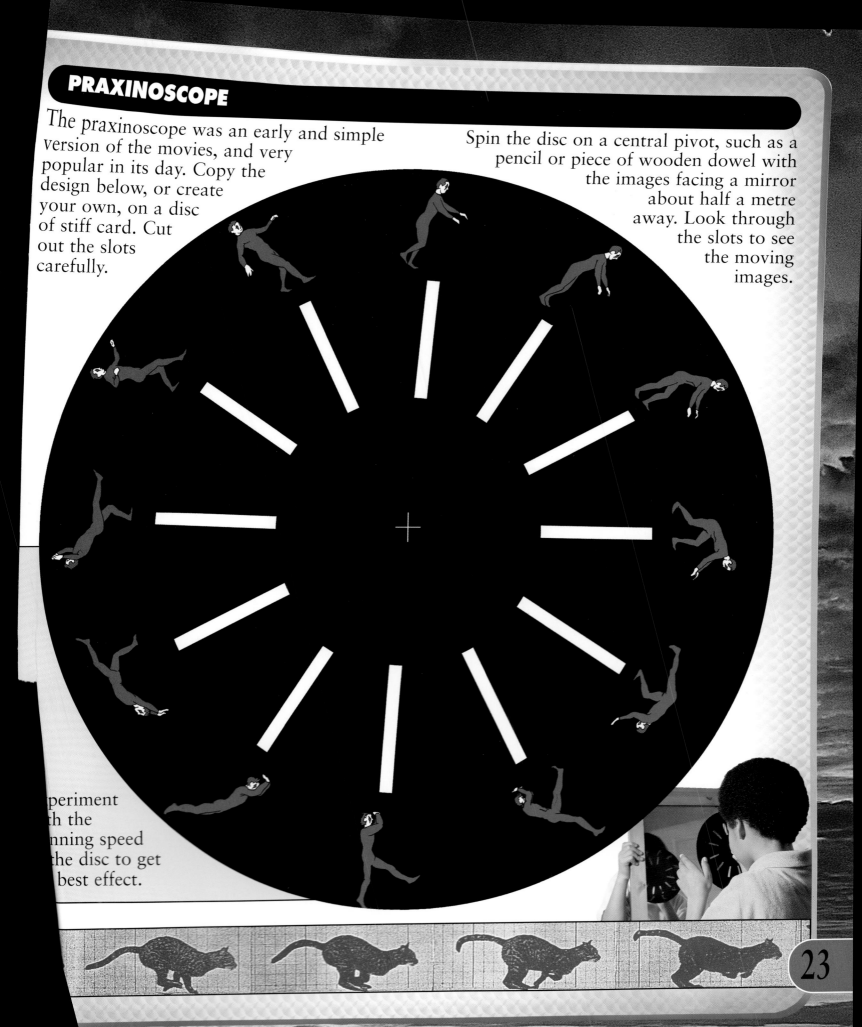

periment
th the
nning speed
the disc to get
best effect.

Laser light is a special kind of light. It has more energy than ordinary light, is brighter, stays as a narrow beam for longer, and shines farther. Laser light has hundreds of uses in today's world.

SCANS AND SCALPELS

In a CD (compact disc) or DVD (digital versatile disc) player, a low-power laser beam shines at the underside of the disc. It detects microscopic pits in the surface and makes electrical signals, which are a digital version of the sounds, pictures or other information on the disc. In supermarkets and stores, low-power red lasers scan bar codes to identify products and prices. In medicine, laser scalpels work like ultra-sharp blades to cut into parts of the body, even the eye, with great accuracy.

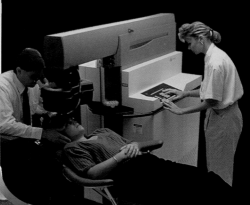

Laser surgery can be used to improve sight.

In industry, very powerful laser beams can cut plastics and even solid metals quickly and with great precision.

Ex
wi
spi
of
the

How it WORKS

In ordinary light the waves are different wavelengths, giving a mixture of colours. Also the waves do not rise and fall in step with each other, and they spread out slightly.

In laser light the waves are all the same length, giving a single pure colour. Also their peaks are all lined up together, and the waves do not spread out but stay parallel.

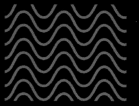

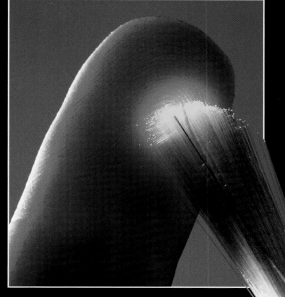

LASER COMMUNICATIONS

Ordinary wires carry information as codes of electrical signals. Optical fibres carry information as coded pulses of laser light. The fibres are rods of a transparent substance, usually special glass, which are thinner than hairs. Millions of pulses can be sent along each optical fibre every second, carrying thousands of times more information than an electrical wire.

In communication cables, thousands of optical fibres are grouped into bundles and carry vast amounts of information, from telephone calls to television channels.

A hologram is a flat image with three dimensions. The picture alters depending on the angle of your view. It is made by splitting a laser beam. One part shines on to the object and is reflected on to special photographic film, while the other shines directly on the film.

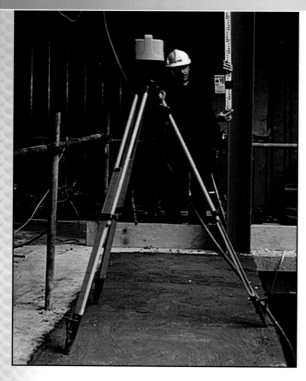

Laser measurers save huge amounts of time, compared to stretching a marked tape along the distance to be measured.

Almost every year sees new devices and gadgets which use light, especially lasers, or a similar form of electromagnetic radiation, such as infrared or microwaves. Imagine a world without the TV remote control!

ULTIMATE PRECISION

Light waves are very, very short, with tens of thousands packed into one millimetre. This means they are useful for very precise measurements. Laser tape measures or rulers send a beam which hits a sensor or bounces back. The time it takes for special pulses within the beam to travel is then measured. A calculation of the distance is made based on the speed of light.

A laser mouse for a computer takes very accurate measurements so that precise movements can be made across the screen.

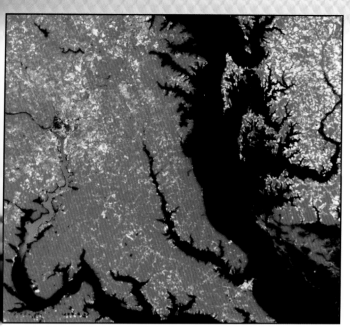

Warm objects like human bodies give off heat as infrared rays. These can be detected by a PIR or passive infrared sensor. PIRs can be used to switch on lights or other equipment as people come near.

INVISIBLE WAVES

Infrared waves are slightly longer than light waves, with tens or hundreds in one millimetre. We cannot see them, but as with light, they can be focused, reflected and carry information as coded pulses.

The temperature difference between land and sea shows up on this infrared image of Chesapeake Bay, taken by a satellite.

TESTING AN INFRARED BEAM

Many remote controllers use infrared. Try pointing a remote control away from its equipment so it does not work. Then try using a mirror to reflect the beam towards the equipment. You can also try using the beam through a dust, like flour, and again through a solid object.

How it **WORKS**

The remote control sends out waves of infrared energy. These waves can be reflected off a mirror, just like a light ray, and they are stronger than light through dust particles. However, infrared still does not work through solid objects.

Dust

Mirror

Solid object

An infrared image of the stars shows that infrared rays pass through dust particles better than normal light. A normal light image of this area would only show up a few dots.

The energy in light can be captured and changed, or transformed, into many other forms of energy. We see this every time we look at plants. They use light energy to grow.

LIVING ON LIGHT

A plant's leaves take in light energy and use it to join together two simple substances – water sucked up through roots from the ground, and carbon dioxide gas taken in from the air. The result is sugar, which contains lots of energy. This is used as food by the plant for its life processes, and to grow and make flowers and seeds. The process is known as photosynthesis, 'building with light'.

How it WORKS

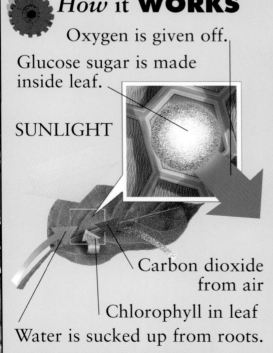

Oxygen is given off.

Glucose sugar is made inside leaf.

SUNLIGHT

Carbon dioxide from air

Chlorophyll in leaf

Water is sucked up from roots.

KEPT IN THE DARK

Many plants start to grow underground, but soon after the seeds have sprouted, they need light. Sow some cress seeds on damp blotting paper in a box. Cut a shape in the lid to allow light to shine on to certain seeds. Put the box in a well-lit area for a few days. The seeds with light should grow well, while those in the dark will not. The result is a 'living pattern'.

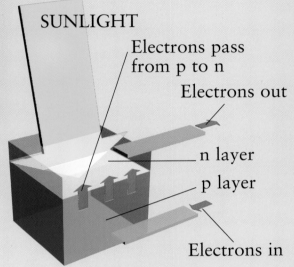
A typical solar cell produces about 1.5 volts. Many solar cells can be grouped together in solar panels or arrays, for larger amounts of electricity.

Communications satellites use solar panels to make enough power to keep their electronic equipment working while they are in space.

LIGHT TO ELECTRICITY

Devices called solar cells take in light energy and convert it to electricity. Their more accurate name is photovoltaic cells. The light energy makes tiny parts of atoms called electrons jump from one place to another, and a stream of many moving electrons forms an electric current. The electricity that solar cells produce can be stored in batteries and used later, such as for lights when it goes dark.

Solar cells are used to power many small electrical gadgets, such as calculators and radios.

THE NATURE OF LIGHT

Light is a form of electromagnetism – a combination of electrical and magnetic energy. It moves or propagates in straight lines unless obstructed by an object or substance. Light can be imagined as travelling in up-and-down waves or as a stream of tiny particles which are 'packets of energy' known as photons.

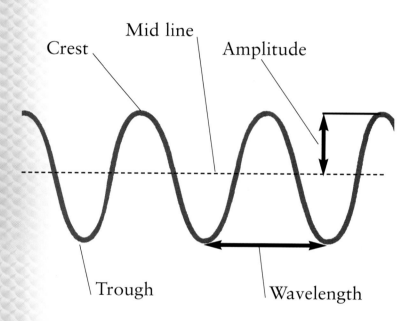

Mid line
Crest
Amplitude
Trough
Wavelength

WAVELENGTH

Wavelength of light varies according to its colour. Longest are red light waves at one end of the spectrum, 770 nm (nanometres). This means about 1300 waves fit into one millimetre. Green waves have medium length and the shortest are violet, at 400 nm.

FREQUENCY

Frequency is a measure of how many waves go past per second and is measured in Hz (Hertz). As wavelength decreases, more pass each second, so frequency increases. The average frequency of all colours in 'white' light is 10 million billion Hz.

BRIGHTNESS

The brightness of light is measured in various ways. The amount of light energy given out by an object is known as the candela (cd):
• Bright LED on electronic gadget – 5 cd
• 100W electric light bulb – 180 cd when viewed from the side, 70 cd when viewed from the end.
• Car headlamp beam – 100,000 cd
• Bright torch beam at 1 metre – 1 million cd

SPEED OF LIGHT

The speed of light through a vacuum, such as space, is 299,792 km/sec. At this speed light could travel:
• Across the Atlantic Ocean in 1/70th of a second.
• Around the world 7 times in less than a second.
• To the Moon in just over 1 second.
• From the Sun in 8 minutes.
• To Proxima Centauri, our next-nearest star after the Sun, in 4.2 years. A light-year is how far light travels in one year – 9.46 million million km.

LIGHT SPEED

Light has the fastest possible speed of all in a vacuum (see panel). When passing through substances it travels more slowly, depending on the density of the substance:
• Air   299,700 km/sec
• Water   225,000 km/sec
• Window glass   195,000 km/sec
• Decorative (crystal) glass   160,000 km/sec
• Diamond   125,000 km/sec

GLOSSARY

focal length
The distance from the centre of a lens or mirror, to where it makes light rays come to a focus (see entry below).

focus
When light or similar rays are reflected or refracted, so that they merge at a certain place and form a clear and sharp image, rather than a blurred one.

hologram
An image that has only two dimensions, height and width – yet seems to have the third dimension of depth too.

lens
A shaped piece of clear glass or plastic, which refracts light rays to change the view of an object seen through it.

optical
To do with light – the science of light is known as optics.

photosynthesis
The process by which green plants use the energy in sunlight to turn carbon dioxide and water into energy-rich foods, especially sugar.

pigment
A substance that is used to give colour to glass, paints, inks, cloth and similar materials.

pixel
'Picture element', the smallest part or unit of an image – usually on a screen – which can be controlled and altered. Many pixels make up the whole image.

reflect
To bounce back, as when sound waves bounce off a wall as an echo, or light rays reflect off a mirror to form an image.

refract
To bend or change direction, as when light rays bend as they pass into or out of a glass object.